Teachings From Experience

Written by:
Hal Bassow

Cadmus Publishing
www.cadmuspublishing.com

Copyright © 2022 Hal Bassow

Published by Cadmus Publishing
www.cadmuspublishing.com
Port Angeles, WA

ISBN: 978-1-63751-171-8

All rights reserved. Copyright under Berne Copyright Convention, Universal Copyright Convention, and Pan-American Copyright Convention. No part of this book may be reproduced, stored in a retrieval system, or transmitted in any form, or by any means, electronic, mechanical, photocopying, recording or otherwise, without prior permission of the author.

From the Author

I am putting this book together so that you can have the best recovery possible. I know what it means to be in recovery from all your mental health issues. I myself suffer from depression issues and also from PTSD. I am living my life in a mental health hospital. I have had many struggles throughout my recovery but I can tell you each of us has a story to tell about our recovery. The journey has taken us to a place where we had up's and down's in our lives. As mental health patients we have been worried about our own recovery and sometimes we do good in our path to getting well. Other times, we have not. I hope this book will help you on your path to recovery, forever.

Day 1

I hope this is your moment that you want to change in your recovery. Do not be sidelined by anything that will take you from your journey to success. You have it in you to do this. Know that nobody can stop you from this moment. People may say things about you but never let it get you down. Put your best foot forward and let your dreams come true. Let the wonderful sun shine in your life. God loves you and the blessings are for you.

Positive Words

Live in the moment taking it one day at a time. As you take it one day at a time, you will see the things you are capable of doing in your journey to a better you.

Hal Bassow

Day 2

Be the man or woman you want to be. Never be afraid to ask the tough questions about your mental health issues. This is your time to blossom into a flower. It grows and turns into a bud, then into a big flower. Recover is just like that.

Positive Words

This is your time to make the best out of your recovery. Now is a great time to start from this day forward doing what makes you happy in your life. You can do it from now and into the future and beyond. Do not let your emotions get the best of you.

Hal Bassow

Day 3

Just as we go on living a somewhat normal lifestyle, we try to be well. If we cannot stop our bad habits, then how are we going to see the path to recovery happen. Just like that flower, we start small, then go big. So often, we tell ourselves we can never be normal but who cares as long as we learn that our mental health issues are real. That is half the battle. We have to have times where we can just laugh and just be ourselves. We all have tough days to go through but we can shine on to a better day of happiness.

Positive Words

Do not let anyone go without you. In their lives, they need you so live on, you have a lot to give to this world.

HAL BASSOW

Day 4

Today, start your year off with a bang. Strive to do better in your life. Do be afraid to fall down, but learn to pick yourself back up. There is a light at the end of the road. SO, go out and reach it. Because just like that light, you shine bright in everything you do.

Positive Words

When you feel things are not going the way you want them to, then take a different approach to the problem at hand. If you are feeling like giving up, well do not because things will work out for the better.

HAL BASSOW

Day 5

When getting yourself all worked up and all stressed out and ready to lose your shit while everything is going to fall apart, find a way to talk to somebody ASAP rather than acting out. Be calm and get yourself in a better place and figure out the problem that is causing you to stress out. It is alright to ask for help when these moments come up. For me, when I get these stressed out moments, I used to act on them, but now I have learned to handle them differently than how I used to react on my negative thoughts. But at times, I hope you have it in you to do better as these thoughts arise in your mind. Some of you may feel like the hell with everything, I do not care any more about anything. This is not the way to think. It is just a totally wrong way of thinking.

Positive Words

You got this. Staying on track and finding a way back to your best, you right now you know yourself better than anyone in your life, or do you?

Hal Bassow

Day 6

How often do you ask yourself the question of who am I and how did I get to be this way and what makes me do what I do in my life. Well, that is a question you will have to find out as you go through your journey to recovery. There is no bad trait in you or bad genes, you simply misused them.

Positive Words

Be who you want to be: a great singer, a great writer, or just a good person with a heart to want to see yourself and others succeed.

Day 7

Time to get a makeover – not that kind of makeover, ladies – change your thoughts to change your ways. Look at your life and the way you think and then personally decide if you want to make the necessary changes in it. What becomes noticeable is the way you handle difficult/uncomfortable situations among others. This could be changing your daily outlooks about yourself or just changing your life style of living. Now that is how you make change.

Positive Words

Be at your best. Do not let the small things get in your way. Move past it, you have bigger fish to fry.

Day 8

You need to let yourself sit back for a while and take a look at your past choices. Your background and your family history may be used to pinpoint why you are the way you are: criminal activity, anger, violence, etc. Then you notice that by simply becoming aware of these attributes you can apply them appropriately to your future self. Looking back at your past can be a good thing for some people, but if it brings up any old trauma, then seek professional help right away.

Positive Words

Figure out how you want to change your ways for the greater good. That is in you. Yes, change is good, oh yes it is.

Hal Bassow

Day 9

Having self-awareness can help you see yourself for who you are, and then target the areas of your life which are causing you problems. Your self-help rehabilitation your weak areas. There is no quality that you possess which is bad; you simply misunderstand them. Oh, and stop blaming others for your own problems. Your problems are your problems, so deal with them.

Positive Words

Do not feel bad about how your life is going. Try and fix it for a better tomorrow. Life is a bitch, but you do not have to be one. So don't. Be good at learning your faults and fix them for the future.

Day 10

Setting your goals and making them achievable is necessary. Starting out small is the key when it comes to obtaining your goals successfully. Try to set the goals you want to set for yourself. I've learned you can have much success by following through with all your long- and short-term goals. Small goals should be first then second for the big ones.

Positive Words

Be a goal setter. Start small then go big at your goals. You got this, goals setter.

HAL BASSOW

Day 11

The background behind why we do see things in a negative way. In this book, you will learn how to become better at helping yourself and others. You will learn how to tackle the frustrating situations your encounter, in your recovery. You will also see improvement and you will begin to think outside the box.

Positive Words

Be a bigger person when it comes to getting angry at someone. You know yourself well enough so think before you do anything.

Day 12

Do not stop being a leader in every way possible so you can pass on positive vibes to someone else in your life. This has worked for me, and I hope this will work for you as you continue to improve in your recovery. If you can be a way to walk out of the darkness in your recovery, then as you move past all the haters, you can then just be yourself. No judgment here.

Positive Words

Do not let the haters get you down. You are too good for that. And do not fall off that path to your successful recovery.

Day 13

We say too often that we cannot trust the doctor who has care over our treatment; we need to stop and let these people help us in our daily lives, whether it has got to do with them having us take medication or therapy. I myself had a lot of time to get well. You know that anything is possible. Do not limit yourself. It is hard to put your trust in people and hope they are here for the right reasons, but as said before, we need to open our circle of trust up. Believe me, I know what I am saying, I have been there.

Positive Words

Stay well. Be well. This is your time to build a great circle of trust of people who are in your corner that care for you and your journey to success.

Day 14

Stop and think for a moment: Do I want to be a follower or a leader in the pack of wolves? We always do before we think and that is what leads us into trouble and then we lose sight of the big picture when things do not go our way. We need to know that we only hurt our own selves by doing more damage than fixing the problem. Do yourself a favor and do not burn bridges and do not bite the hand that feeds you.

Positive Words

Be a leader, not a follower in your life. The only way you really see change is by making change happen in your future.

Hal Bassow

Day 15

Sometimes it can be hard to use our breathing and visualization exercises. We feel at times that we do not need to use them. I can tell you firsthand, this exercise is working for me. I know it can work for you. Figure out a breathing visualization exercise to do with your therapist or your treatment provider who has direct care over you. Visualization exercises can be a good way for you to visualize a happy place in your past or present. The journey is the destination. You are already at the finish line, you made it; do not turn or look back now. You just put on your new self. It is time to stay on the right path.

Positive Words

We try too often to deny the fact that we do not have a mental health problem at all, but it is time for us to stop living in denial and know that if we cannot be real with ourselves, then how are we going to be real with others around us.

Day 16

As hard as it may sound, do not give up on yourself now. It is not the time to melt down and throw in the towel because we cannot get what we want in our treatment services. We need to just sit back and let the professionals take it from here. Stop trying to be someone you are not and let those people figure out what is the best course of action we need in our treatment. Do not panic; we just need to accept the fact that these professionals want to help us with our recovery.

Positive Words

Accepting that we do have a major problem is half the battle because sometimes we try to avoid the fact that there is something wrong with us.

Day 17

My therapist once told me that you have to stop talking and let someone else get a word in at times. When you are trying to figure out your problems or just to solve them. We cannot get to the root of the problems unless we let the other person respond back with an answer to our major issues. That is why it is so important to let others talk first and we just need the lesson. We are our worst enemy and we just do not know it. Be a person that wants to let others help us. We cannot do this alone, so do not ever try it. I know this because I have seen it happen a lot throughout my own recovery. Then, as we give in and show who we really are. Not in a bad way, but more in a good way, trying to make sense of it all. It is hard to do so I would like to tell you to let the therapist help us on our path. They're the best resource to go when things get rough.

Positive Words

Do not try to be your own worst enemy. You will not even know it is happening until it is too late.

Hal Bassow

Day 18

Our recovery is like a pogo stick, bouncing up and down. We need to find that balance in our treatment because our racing thoughts get the best of us. It takes us to unhappy places in our mind, but if we focus on people who care for us, there is no reason to take everything so seriously because after all, we are better than that.

Positive Words

Really try not to be so serious. Be free from fear.

Day 19

If you commit a crime and you know you are guilty, just own up to your shit. Do not be that person who said, "Nope, not me, I did not do it," but knowing damn well you did it. Then, just confess as it is said in the Bible. The truth shall set you free. So, forgive yourself and the victim and move forward from the pain it may be causing, you have remorse. Confess your sins and let God or your higher power and anyone in your life that matters come into your heart. Trust me, you will feel much better. The truth has set me free and I know it can set you free. So tell yourself that I do not want to keep the burden of guilt with one for the rest of my life. So, do yourself and others a favor and be better than your criminal mindset.

Positive Words

Say to yourself these words, "I was wrong," and take responsibility for the things I have done. I know I can do better in my life.

Day 20

Sometimes people make an ass of themselves and look stupid afterwards trying to know how tough they are to someone else trying to be the alpha male. Do not be that person. Be your true self. Be a lover, not a fighter. Pretending to be someone you are not will only hurt you. So be the good guy from here on out because the alpha male is really a soft, kind-hearted person deep down inside. A person's personality is key to how a person presents themselves.

Positive Words

People say a man is not supposed to cry. Then, if you do not, then you are not a man—you are being someone people want you to be, not your true self of being who you want to be.

HAL BASSOW

Day 21

We are not getting any younger, but we are getting wiser and much more mature, so do not let anything that is going to hold you back get in the way of your future self. It is time to do for you and your circle of people you hang out with in your lifetime. Be smarter in every way possible. That is how you see yourself and the journey to recover comes to a great end of the road. After reading this book, learn to help others and yourself; do just what makes you happy in life such as going to a good job or going back to school is something that gave me a sense of pride and I know it can give you a sense of pride, too. So, as I said before, rock on with yourself.

Positive Words

I know you have had many hardships over the last few years. Now I bet you can tell yourself you have gotten to a better place after this and staying true to yourself.

Day 22

When I first started doing drugs and drinking, I was very young. I did not know what damages it could have cost me. I was 13 when I started smoking pot; but as I got older, I did the heavy stuff like Angel Dust and Black 'N Milds and drinking booze, plus Newport 100s. My family only knew I was doing pot, if you want to change yourself, then you have to find it in yourself to get help right away. Leave the bad memories behind. Be a person who wants help from the substance use disorders. If you have these problems, then really seek help before you do something you will regret. We all are or have been destroying the ones we love.

Positive Words

Do not let yourself get to the point where you do so many drugs it costs you your freedom. As it did for this author.

Day 23

I have had a lot to think about these last few years. My last few years have been dark for me, but I have grown to show everyone I have become a better man. The young look up to me. And if you have someone that looks up to you, then you need to not let them down. It can be hard to live in our darkest hour, but no matter what there are a lot of people who really care for us and our wellbeing. We just have to open our eyes up to see who is really here for us. Do not stop being your true self no matter what anyone tells you.

Positive Words

If you could talk to your younger self, what would you tell him/her? I would say to tell him to make better choices and not to make the same mistakes I have made in my past. Stop trying to be in the spotlight.

Day 24

Have an open mindset. Do not get off track. Your journey is a long haul, but you can make it possible to achieve it so do not let your guard down. You have in you to do better in your treatment by following the treatment provider's orders. You can have the best possible future.

Positive Words

Follow everything the treatment providers have for you. Doing this will definitely help you improve your ways having a difficult time, then stop and figure out what are the difficulties you are having at the moment and ask questions. Do not be afraid to be a question asker.

Day 25

Sometimes it can be hard to hold our tongue from what you really want to say, so why don't we do better at speaking our mind when we feel that we need to stand up for ourselves. It's okay to tell someone to back off and leave you alone. If you don't stand up to the person that is bothering you then they will never stop harassing you; so say these words to them: "Back off. Leave me the hell alone. Get out of my face. You don't put fear in me." As you say these words, mean it. Take it to heart. If they put hands on you, then seek help from someone else and leave the area right away. Being a bigger person is always a good thing because no matter what, you will always come out the winner in any situation. Look, I get it – this may seem so corny, but really: am I wrong?

Positive Words

Put your foot down. Stand tall in everything you do. Don't be pushed around by anyone. Let them know you are serious and are not playing games with them. Doing this will let them know you are not to be messed with. As people in recovery may not understand, but we can't keep letting others walk all over us. It's time to stand up and get out of being in fear. Let's stop people from taking advantage of us.

Day 26

We dealt with a lot of judgment in our mental health journey. People who really don't know what we are feeling or how they are trying so hard to get an understanding about us. But I will say this again: if those treatment providers don't have experience with your issue, then you hold back from expressing your true self because you don't think they have your best interest at heart. But no matter what. Be open with and them remember they are there to advocate and support you, not always getting on you for the most judgmental behaviors they feel you are doing. Look, having mental health disorders can be tough. People not wanting to accept us for who we are because we have a problem in their eyes. But if they can't accept you for who you are, then who are they really? You need people who are going to be in your corner, trying to have your best interest at heart, wanting to see you get to that journey to recovery path. As I said before, no judgment here or at any time in this book, so be open with yourself. Don't be afraid to say what you really want to say, but say it in as few words as possible so you get direct and straight to the point, so you get what you want out of the conversation in a positive manner.

Positive Words

If people are judging you because you have a mental health disorder, then pay them no mind. You're better than that. Don't get all caught up in other people's drama. Focus on your path to the destination to success in this lifetime expressed in your own life.

Teachings from Experience

Hal Bassow

Day 27

People such as ourselves have a bad way of thinking sometimes. It gets the most out of us and takes us a long time to do the best thing that keeps us on our path to behaving in a manner that doe no harm to ourselves or damages others. We need to start this day forward thinking more positive. Having others and ourselves thinking positive is not a bad thing at all; it's really a good thing. Because acting and being positive will keep you on the straight path. Can't fail till you try, because failing is a part of growing as a person in life. Try not to be looking so mad all the time. Try smiling for once throughout your daily life.

Positive Words

Be positive, stay positive. Trust me, I started to be more positive and it's working. So why don't you give it a try? It's the best thing ever. You might not even know it. As I learned to stay positive, I've learned to change my behavior. So can you. As you change your negative thinking others may see how positive you've become. Maybe they may want to become more positive about their own lives. So be that leader in the pack of wolves— it's really not that hard.

Day 28

Losing a loved one is so painful to deal with. Trust me, I know this because I lost so many people in my own life. At times I did not know what to do with myself. I felt like I lost the people who kept me having a life in the way I did. Some of it was as crazy as childhood and adulthood, but for the most part I learned life is too short to stay upset with the one you lost in your life. I would say live and let go. Figure out how you can tell someone what you are feeling and how it's effecting your life in this present moment. Stay strong for yourself and the ones that are around you at this moment.

Positive Words

Ask yourself the tough question: Can I keep living my life the way I'm living in the sorrow for the rest of my days on this earth. Decide who you want to be moving forward. Faith comes from within no matter what kind of faith you believe in. Take your time. You are more powerful than you know.

Day 29

Change your behavior before it gets worse. The thing I've taught myself today in this present time is to change my old bad behavior to new ways of behaving so I can live a better life from here on out. You don't want to have to keep making the same mistakes for the rest of your life. You have it in you to make the necessary changes you need to make to help your journey to recovery. Don't limit yourself. You're better than that at this time.

Positive Words

Never let anyone tell you that you can't be who you want to be. If you can think it or dream it, you can make it a reality. Just let your dreams come true. That's the best way to live a positive lifestyle. Never forget that you are special in everything you do. You're not a fool, you're a person with feelings who wants to do big things in this world.

Day 30

Sometimes you think you have to go 0 to 100 on someone because they did you wrong, but you have to be a better person and not let them get the best of you. Going 0 to 100 is not the answer if I must say. Talk it out first. I know this sounds so lame. When you are upset with somebody or just angry at them. If talking it out does not work, then you must find a different way to deal with your issues. When you put your mind, body, and soul into something, nothing is impossible. That is right: nothing.

Positive Words

Here is where the book ends, but read it over and over so you see yourself doing better at things. Remember, the journey is the destination. By for now. See you in the book.

Bonus Page 1

The truth is, others may try to predict your future. But only you can determine what your destiny will be like. For as long as you can remember, you have a concern to want to help others closest to you. But yes, it is said, how can you help others if you can't help yourself. But you know what? As long as you know that your problems won't take control of your life and you have worked to better control how you present yourself to others. But really, is there something wrong with helping people as well as yourself? Because in the long run, the person you are helping you and them can strive to do great things in this lifetime, getting and making sure you get and stay well. Sometimes we are quick to blame others; when we know that we have done wrong reality sets in, right now. The truth always comes to light no matter how long you hide or run away from your wrong doings. Lesson when you get out of the denial phase, you'll begin to see real success. It's normal to not want to hear the truth. Why get because the truth hurts. Instead of blaming others for your faults, just be real with yourself because that's the only way you see change occur. Take a moment to look at yourself and own up to your wrong-doings.

Bonus Page 2

Young people cope with family stress just like dealing with the stress of mental health issues and trying to cope with how to handle and get a grip on your mental health. Look, the reality is teens have to cope with the same stresses as adults do. You have to find strategies and long-term skills for resolving your conflicts. Just getting started can be the scariest thing to do because we feel like we have to keep everything inside our head for the rest of our life and just live with the pain. No, not true. You can get rid of the sorrow/bad behavior out of your mind by taking the time to talk with someone you feel okay talking to who's in your corner. Look, the real madness is we're told to just deal with all the stress building up in us. Deal with it, then they really are not here for you because recognizing your own signs of trouble related to your stress is key – and yes, I would say handling it can be overwhelming so don't try to do it or handle it by yourself, you may get lost in your head trying to combat stress in life. It's confusing. Yes, that's right, confusing. As I always would say, you will not understand solving bad emotions on your own without having another set of eyes and ears from someone who maybe can help you solve the major issues you face. Because as young people do get it, dealing with problems on your own can affect your adulthood. Thinking you know everything because you want to act grown. Just stop. Be good at learning from your faults.

Hal Bassow

Bonus Page 3

Look, we need to know when to just say no to others and not get all trapped in a web of lies by just trying to please others because we want to try to fit in. You don't have to please anyone. They're not true friends if they want you to do things you know are wrong just to be down with the bad group of people stopping you from your success in your future. So don't be the person who just wants to look cool to others, like smoking pot or tobacco. Really, for this author, I should have told my younger self these things and maybe I would have never done any drugs or alcohol. I should have listened to my family, the ones who have been there before and learned from their mistakes when they were young. Here's what I would say: try to develop a better way to handle your anger towards others around you. Look, I get it. Peer pressure can be one of the most difficult things to walk away from when you're trying to impress friends. But when things get out of control, police get involved. Where are those friends when you go downtown for doing something you know your parents have raised you better. So what now? No one to turn to but family. Why you're so quick to call your loved ones is because you know family never leaves you hanging for dead. But if your family wants to show you a lesson or two and tell you 'I told you so,' and then you say I'm sorry. To be direct, just say no to peer pressure. After all, you learn from your wrong doings and you become much more wise.

Teachings from Experience

Bonus Page 4

As you walk the thin line between hell in a cell, when everything is failing or going in the wrong direction and not going the way you want them to, I hope that if you can let all the hardships go and focus on what needs to happen to get you to the point where you can tell yourself and others who care about your recovery. I am at the end of my negative thinking. I've found new ways to move past that type of thinking. I have new ways of acting/thinking. After reading this book, I also understand my road to recovery is a long haul. It's never ending. It doesn't mean I can't change my ways, handling my negative issues. You can say I got to this point with the help of others and my self-help, rehabilitation. Again, I hope this inspirational book has given you a sense that even though we may have mental health issues, we can do anything if we put our minds to it. So live on with your true self.

Positive Words

Always be ready to be honest with yourself and others who have a close relationship with you within your mental health treatment. Don't lose control. Now you know yourself well enough, so please don't give up hope or what you have as beliefs in life because as said in the main days of this book, you can shine on to a better day of happiness. It's true. So why not be happy? Trust me, it will benefit you for the better; you know it and I know it let's make it happen.

Teachings from Experience

HAL BASSOW

Bonus Page 5

Let's change our lives, get out of our heads, and live better than we ever did before. What's better than that, right? So let's do it. Why? Because you know it's the right thing to do. Just say no to others who don't want you to do good things with yourself. You know deep inside you want the best for your life. You have probably dreamed of having the ability to make the necessary changes that will promote success in your recovery.

Fear is one of the most powerful weapons that keeps you from achieving true success, if I must say so. First things first. You need to stay self-motivated as mental health patients. There are opportunities out there for us, so don't be in fear of anything. You want to know something? Satan loves fear. He eats you alive. He smells fear. That's one of the ways he gets you caught up in the mess you're in. SO just be free from fear and the lies you've been told about yourself that you can't do something or have any opportunities because you're mentally ill. Not true. You can have the same success and opportunities others around you have. Yes, you can. You want it, then just put the work in to get there. It may be hard or easier said than done, but you can make it happen. We are quite the characters. We've been selling ourselves our whole lives – it's time to make the best move that's right for us. Don't be so hard on yourself. Don't give up now. Stop wasting time and let fear go out the window. Trash your old self here to the new!

HAL BASSOW

Bonus Page 6

By reading this book to the very end is proof that you want to change yourself and achieve personal growth and better self help your negative thinking. How to approach things in a positive way while you are still in recovery or in a hospital for your mental health issues, or rehab center for substance abuse problems. Once let out in the free world, along with this, again you get rid of your criminal mindset as well as your negative choices that led to all the wrongful thinking in your life. I hope this book gave you the opportunity to think outside the box and act positive, so you can show family and friends you're working towards positive endeavors, letting them know you are trying to change your ways of acting. Best of luck with your positive endeavors and getting rid of your criminal mindset. Look, many people such as ourselves are seeking to get educated about our major issues affecting our substance use disorders. Behind walls we struggle to realize our dream of attaining an education, but the struggle is not due to our abilities or ambition, but rather to. People telling you that you can't' do it because they don't think you have the skill or abilities.

ABOUT THE AUTHOR

My name is Hal James Bassow, but I was born into this world as Harold James Lewis III on July 8, 1991. Some would call me a summer baby. If you must know, yes, I had a change of name not to walk away or hide from anything. Let's start by telling you why I changed it. Well, it is because my father passed away when I was only one year old. So, I never got the chance to meet him. My father's two sisters were very phony. They were always saying how they wanted to be part of my life after my father passed, but any time I try to reach out to them, they would shut me out or blame everything on my mother for them not being able to see me. I had a sister from my father's side. She is way older than me. She never shut me out because family don't turn away from family, no matter what. You stand by your loved ones.

I was born in Hartford, Connecticut to my mother, Selma, who raised me and my sister and brother. My step-father came into my life when I was very young. He was a good person in our life, always trying to make sure we had the best childhood we could have. We really never suffered at all because he was around and taught me a lot of life lessons. Don't get me wrong, I walked away from everyone and was doing things I thought were the right things in my own life to do. When I was young, a real evil man assaulted me sexually. My mother had him staying with us in the house so he could get on his feet. I did not tell my mother because I was scared of him. I will never forget what happened. People may say things about me. How I was a shy kid always wanting to be around my mother or hang with the women rather than the guys. I hung out with the wrong crowd, getting into a lot of trouble doing all of the things I should have never been doing, but I was young and very stupid, breaking all the rules with my gang members. I was smoking pot and using heavy stuff like angel dust, drinking alcohol when I could get to it or if I had someone at the right age who would buy it. Someone who was not a family member because my family never approved of things like that. A troubled kid trying to shove all the pain away, under the rug, but the pain was still with me because it is hard for me to open up to anyone about my life. As I sit here and write this "About the Author" page, I feel comfortable talking about what I dealt with in my own life, but it's time for me to be real with myself and others around me. I always would say putting on a front for someone else trying to be something you are not will only hurt you in the long run, but being true to yourself now there's nothing wrong with that.

At this point in my life, I left the gang life. I got a cool quick gig going door to door working for Positive Energy as an authorized field agent relly rell, the fucking boss had him a nine to five. There as time went on I was the highest paid agent. At Positive at my job I became a branch manager that is where I tell you of how I met the woman of my dreams. She was walking downtown past the branch and I spotted her as I was standing outside waiting to go out in the field with the other agents. I had to walk up to her and talk because when I see beauty in a woman, I must speak. She was the most amazing person I have ever seen in my life. She had a six year old son, Julian, my step-son, who I raised like he was my own kid. The way I was taught was that if you meet or get into a relationship with somebody and start a family with them and they already have kids of their own, you don't disown them and just do for the mother. It's a package deal, you do for everyone – that's what a real man does. That's what I learned being around my step-father.

Me and, Alicia, we did so much together. I could talk to her about anything I wanted because she was my Ride to Die girl. I was always there for them any time of day or night. Julian looked up to me as his father because his real father used to beat him and his mother. So after some time, the father went to prison and soon after I stepped into their lives. As Alicia would say, you're the best man that loved me and my son who said it's OK, I'm here now. No one will ever harm you or your son ever again. Julian was my li'l guy. I gave him the nickname Li'l Wise.

I miss them so much that I hate myself every time I look in the mirror. I broke my promise to Julian when I said I will always be there for you. I always told him never let any man put fear in your heart, but for me. When I was young, yes, I let a man put fear in my heart, but as I got older, I told myself that won't happen again. But needless to say that promise I did not keep because I got locked up. Alicia and I were supposed to get married and we planned on hopefully having a daughter.

I lost everything in my life after coming into the hospital. I lost the woman of my dreams. The woman I loved to death was gone just like that. She did not want anything to do with me anymore. She left December 25, 2012, on Christmas Day. That's why I hate that day when it comes around every year. She called me while I was here in the hospital. She said there's too much "he said, she said" stuff going around. I can't do this anymore, so me and Julian, we have to move on with our lives and you should too.

I did not know what to do with myself. I lost all respect for myself, I was sent to the psych-hospital for a crime to which I had to confess for I was truly, guilty. What made me do it, the immediate cause, was heavy combination of Angel Dust. For many years, I had hid my frustration, fears, hatred, and anger deep down inside. I wasn't ready to admit to other's that I was really didn't have it together. After the crime, I made a decision to get clean after. I almost lost my life. Down by Connecticut – river front, smoking, Angel Dust, and booze for the last time. This was my third blackout, in my life. I took this as a wake-up call from above God. I was lost. Had been from the beginning and never asked anyone for directions. I felt hopeless, guilt-ridden, briming, shame, to my family. And now, facing perhaps years in a mental-institution, I kicked against my cage. My days were marked by rage. Fitful dreams of getting freedom. I sat in my cell and wondered how it would end. All this madness and frustration I felt inside. I tried to end it myself by suicide. But couldn't quite do it. Something inside said, stay alive, you have a lot to give. I forgave myself, have remorse. Because we all have destroyed, or are destroying the one's we care for. I learned to be better then my criminal mindset. I've grown to show everyone I've become a better man. If you are where I've been, or perhaps even in worse conditions. My sincere prayers in that you know true freedom comes from, within with forgiveness comes freedom. As you must know I feel free from all my drug use/criminal-mindset.

This is a short brief clip of the most important aspects of my life. It's not so in-depth because this book is not an autobiography. It is a book for inspiration. It's a positive force of motivation that I hope will help you learn from your mistakes I'm investing my time in this book for me and you.

SO ROCK ON WITH YOURSELF, FROM THE AUTHOR.

Special Thanks

To Melody S. Forensic treatment specialist for encouraging and inspiring me to get back writing my stories. Through her encouragement and belief in me, this book is now in your hands. Let me say thanks to everyone at Cadmus Publishing for helping to make this book become a reality. To my family for standing by me all these years. As I face challenges in the road to recovery also to Sarah for being a great proof-reader.

www.ingramcontent.com/pod-product-compliance
Lightning Source LLC
Chambersburg PA
CBHW071911070526
44583CB00016B/1937